COLD MORNING SKY

THE MACMILLAN COMPANY
NEW YORK · BOSTON · CHICAGO · DALLAS
ATLANTA · SAN FRANCISCO

MACMILLAN AND CO., Limited
LONDON · BOMBAY · CALCUTTA · MADRAS
MELBOURNE

THE MACMILLAN COMPANY
OF CANADA, Limited
TORONTO

COLD MORNING SKY

MARYA
ZATURENSKA

New York
THE MACMILLAN COMPANY
1938

SET UP BY BROWN BROTHERS LINOTYPERS
PRINTED IN THE UNITED STATES OF AMERICA
BY THE FERRIS PRINTING COMPANY

To
MURIEL RUKEYSER

ACKNOWLEDGMENT

Some of these poems have appeared in *Poetry* (Chicago), *Life and Letters To-day* (London), *The Nation*, *The New Republic*, *Smoke*, *The American Mercury*, *New Letters in America*.

I should like to express my thanks for helpful criticism of this manuscript to Mr. Horace Gregory, Mr. Robert Hillyer, Miss Eda Lou Walton, and Mr. T. C. Wilson.

CONTENTS

COLD MORNING SKY

MIDSUMMER NOON

Calm, ripe, and gold the shadows fell
On trees whose green was feather-light
In the sweet air against a sky
Tranced in the rich midsummer spell
Of beauty, warm, compacted, bright,
Glowing in clear intensity.

And in my wrist, and at my brain
The jeweled tick of time and sun
Subsided and grew still again.
I saw the sparkling shadows run
Through glimmering avenues of trees
To exquisite oblivion
And the high pitch of noon was done.

And in my head, my ears, my heart
And in the subtle wrist-pulse clear
I felt a clamorous faintness start,
In intimate and desperate fear
Death's elegant, worn face drew near.

The dwindling shadow of that high
Perfection that had grown complete,
Had drained my joy's deep fountains dry
And left things salt that once were sweet.
The world through shadow softly glowing
Restored itself to its own size,
Restored its lowered love and heat
Into the sun-dilated eyes
And natural quiet softly blowing
Descended on the ripening wheat.

[1]

LULLABY

Ruin falls on blackening skies
And disaster lies in wait
For the heart and for the state,
Loud the voices in the street
Shout unhealing remedies.

Sleep, beloved, while you may:
Heralds of the Augustan day
That arise as you awake
Can consume but never slake
The strong thirst, intense and deep,
For the peace that need not sleep.

Let the lion have his hour,
Let the evil beasts devour
Leaf and vine and fruit and flower,
Theirs the night but yours the time
Known to the Vergilian rhyme
When the ancient world, distressed,
Found peace in an infant's breast.

Still remote and gay and young
Sing the stars in ancient peace,
Heralding the great release
In their wordless tongue.
Close your eyes and let them sing
In the morning that will bring
What strange beasts to haunt the spheres?
Revelations? New-found fears?

Let the old world fall away
As the great beasts leave their prey;
Let the dogs and cats destroy
That which they cannot enjoy.
New as life and death and sleep
Shall the cyclic rivers creep,
Bringing learning, art and thought
New again to be renewed,
Revived, restored, and still uncaught,
The intangible pursued.

Sleep, beloved, in the changes
Light from bright to darkness ranges:
Venus, ocean-young, arises,
Love again the earth surprises
Naked, dreaming, peaceful, free,
Springing from the bitter sea
Of unending destiny.

RARE JOY

Not plucked like stars, flowers from the sky
Are you, rare joy whose artless glance
Makes light and sweet the lover's cry,
Teaches the withered heart to dance,
Lights the glazed eyeballs of the blind
And pours its healing on the mind.

Rare as the tropic birds of light
In northern islands dull with frost
Are you restorer of true sight
And that first early freshness lost
Through troubled years; that goodness caught
In innocence, now always sought.

Crown with white violets the hour
When the clock's pulse grows faint with care,
When beauty weeps within her bower
And sees the fatal, first, gray hair
Among her golden tresses show
And feels time's dimming afterglow.

Dear as an infant's face, as loved
As youngest child, by its fond mother
Outstretch your happy hand ungloved
Soft flesh to awakened flesh, no other
Can stir the arid roots of time
In a perpetual summer clime.

O none like you dear joy can move
The eyes to sun, the limbs to speed
In the quick harmony of love
When anger makes the silence bleed.
Teach, teach, your scholar how to send
The message that seals friend to friend.

WATER AND SHADOW

(AFTER SIR PHILIP SIDNEY)

By the long flow of green and silver water
Rushing in limpid light from savage mountains
I walked beneath the shadow of the mountains
That dimmed with barbaric dark, light-jeweled
waters.

Grandeur and majesty and strength descended
On my right hand and left,—in tones of liquid laugh-
ter.
Sweeter than airy birds, child-laughter, star-de-
scended
Star-pointed joy like children's eyes in laughter.

Ran the bright waters down the savage breast
Of the great mountains, sweetness from the strong
Melting the sombre stone with fountained beauty
Young, sparkling, dancing on the frowning moun-
tains.

And from the mirror of the divided skies
As if flashed from the sun on golden streamers
A child descended, small hands bright with flowers,
The sun-sheen gold on her hair, stars on her azure
frock.

Between the night and bright, the delicate and stark,
She flew to earth, scattering flowers and singing
Always of the long flow of green and silver water
And the barbaric shadow of the mountains.

IN SONG, THE COUNTERSIGN

(IN MEMORIAM: D. H. LAWRENCE)

Again that voice intangible as running light
On half awakened trees in early March,
That voice forgotten, heard reluctantly
In dreams that fear the sun, and waking flee.

The songs of sirens are not half so sweet,
So fraught with secret danger, so beguiling:
Where shall we run? where is that warm retreat?
Where can we stop our eyes and calm our minds?
Oh, singing cease! nor draw our unwilling feet
Through the fleet wilderness, dry-shod on the wild
      sea.

No, let us drown in music and resign
Our hearts, our souls, our loves, to the wide waters,
Following the song that leaves the strong will weak,
The forgotten hope, the disastrous dream to seek
The lost music, life's rich countersign.

Now come the maidens to the water's edge
And throw their wreaths away, they wade in starlight;
Now the young men follow, eager and swift,
Lifting their voices through the dew-damp sedge
And through the heavy woods, the embowered night
One voice, one melody, sweet, drowned and faint
Is cool in summer's heat, in darkness bright.

So are our vanquished bodies cast ashore
And empty are our eyes, empty our arms,
And the sharp raptures in our hearts no more.

Our little deaths are swallowed by the sun;
Our aspirations, longings and alarms
Are drawn into sleep's vast felicity:
Oh, not love's martyrs, or life's victims we.

Recorders on bleak stone, symbols of vaster dreams,
Lovers of love, expounders of the blood
Who breathed and floundered in the living flood
Of fine-drawn liquid air, of flowing light.
The perilous mountains lured us through the night
And the remote white voices far away
Until the day seemed night, the night seemed day
We sink, we drown, in bottomless lost streams.

IMAGES IN LAKE WATER

FOR BRYHER

The tree's sun-glittering arms are bowed
With graceful supplication in lake-water
Metallic-green and musically still,
Float tree and water in one image, solitary and proud,
Till the bird-image joins them and the cloud.

Idly I watch the glimmering lights depart,
So gay falls summer glittering on the lake
And on the dreaming trees, on my transfigured heart
Grown iridescent for a shadow's sake.

Unchanging and transparent solitude
Where mobile waters haunt the enduring dream
That trembles like a lily on the stream,
A troubling whiteness on a heavy green,
A starry-snow-drop on a summer scene.

Imagination colors all our watching mood;
The day contracted to a pool, a tree, a shade
All summer shining in a little space,
And the slow falling of the night delayed
With flowing images in the mind; betrayed
In mirrored silence, my reflected face.   .

The arrowy gold whose winter span
Of life was lost in wind and water
Shed from the sky to waters run
Casting new life upon the water.

From water Love herself arose,
Limbs laved in seawater and sun,
Again her smile dissolves the snow
Hearts bared to flowering of the sun.

O brief and glittering time of joy
When the long thoughts of youth run free
And garlanded the girl and boy
With the young flowers as bright and free.

The dark head and the golden one
Glad in the sun, rose-garlanded
Dream of adventures in the sun
High actions, proud, rose-garlanded.

And from their dreams the laurel grows
While artlessly the tide of love
Circles, expands, contracts, and grows
Through sunlit avenues of love.

The Greek, the natural feet of dawn
Wade in lakewaters, calm the sea
Her footsteps light on the green lawn
Sound like faint signals from the sea.

Gold-streaked the air in luminous flashes
Shadows of trees in water flowing
Nostalgic tears on awakened lashes
Remember joy, its ebbing, flowing.

THE LUNAR TIDES

Danger stalks on such nights, the moon is dangerous:
Why will you walk beneath the compelling lustre
That draws the blood from your unwilling body?
The vampire moon with yellow streams of light
Drains the dim waters, sucks the moist air dry
Casts cloudy spectres on the window pane
The dead arise and walk again.

Oh, love how are we drawn
Into this moon, this face as cold
Remorseless as ambition, chilled with fever
Burning with war that on these lunar tides
Draws all life to its danger; beautiful
It mocks the living glory of the sun
Such golden, flowing motion, dipping in perilous play
Forgets the warm assurances of day.

Resistance dies is plucked so gently from
Our paralyzed wills, we hardly know it gone.
We are surrendered to the moon:
The light compels us, pole-stars to its orbit
We shine in darkness fixed, invisible
Too late for the last withdrawal we are lost
In the intricacies of yellow frost.

Fantasies in the brain, restlessness in the heart
Desire for the unattainable the pure romantic longing
Ruined towers in the air, a yearning toward the sea
For its deep death, so cool, and languorous

These are the favorite symptoms written down
The pressure of the moon on the rare spirit
The wild attraction, and the deep repulsion
The irresistible compulsion.

Dogs bark invisible terror, the trees loom sharply
These ague glamors shake down mortal ill
The wind beloved by lunatics and lovers
Descends and sways the grass, compels the lost
Dishevelled light as sharp as silver daggers
Such light as never from Olympus poured
But dark Judean light sorrowful pain-extolling
And Christian light, the Gothic thunder rolling.

THE DAISY

Having so rich a treasury, so fine a hoard
Of beauty water-bright before my eyes,
I plucked the daisy only, simple and white
In its fringed frock and brooch of innocent gold.

So is all equilibrium restored:
I leave the noontide wealth of richer bloom
To the destroyer, the impatient ravisher;
The intemperate bee, the immoderate bird.

Of all this beauty felt and seen and heard
I can be frugal and devout and plain,
Deprived so long of light and air and grass,
The shyest flower is sweetest to uncover.

How poor I was: and yet no richer lover
Discovered joy so deep in earth and water;
And in the air that fades from blue to pearl,
And in a flower white-frocked like my small daughter.

COLD MORNING SKY

Oh, morning fresh and clear as heavenly light,
Like warmth of love within the unwilling breast,
Sad to be so possessed,
Always the delicate shafts, piercing and bright,
Troubling my rest.

Neither tempestuous now, nor tormented
As when in fragrant, unforgotten air
Of the blood's April, all the world was spent
In passionate discontent,
In rapture and despair.

But like rich gold beat thin into a thread,
Metallic-firm and shadow-fine as thought,
So this new Eros rests his shining head
Upon a book much prized and seldom read,
Glad to be captured, shielded and untaught.

Then, under morning, everlasting morning,
Clear as new joy, cool with expectant breath,
The mystery takes blood, the arriving sun gives warn-
    ing;
The soul within its sheath
Explains, endures, interprets all the bliss,
Once new and unexplained,
The lucid flower is named, the numbered kiss,
The pulse-beat numbered and reduced to this
And nothing is profaned.

But airy-light, oh, fragile, bitter-sweet,
A small bell rings and all enchantment's done
In smallest intervals of expanding dawn
Till quiet fills the eyes, lightens the feet,
Dissolves the wonder, all fulfilled, complete.

DIALOGUE

Voice from the old Hesperides
Suddenly rushing to my mind
Like quick rumor of the wind
Among the autumn-stricken trees.

"My beauty runs to seed
My rotting valor goes
To arm against your foes
In your growing need.

Neither man nor ghost am I
Who have come through deathless will
Neither time nor change can kill
To the chamber where you lie.

While I live in memory
Time will spare the scattered bones
They will rise from the grass, the stones
And the shattered tree.

From the pit and from the snare
From the poison in the blood
From the terror of dulled hair
From the phantom in the wood.

From the chilling of your veins
From the deathworm in your thought
From the falling of the rains
From the solstice and the drought."

[17]

Voice that I loved when young
Now that my earth grows old
Speaks with a stranger tongue
In the wind, in the cold.

Face from a banished tomb that peers
Pale through my window pane
What do you say again
After forgotten years?

"My long shed tears are dry
The dishonors of the tomb
Are locked in a little room
Dissolved in secrecy."

THE ISLAND

"I sacrifice this island unto thee
And all whom I lov'd there, and who lov'd mee."
                                              —DONNE.

I give this island green in the green sea
To underseas of floating memory
Where all I loved and hated lie secure
In iceberg cold, jewel-frozen, diamond-pure
There once a boat with Christ's own banners set
Rose from a mist of cloudy-violet-jet
Against blue mountain-tops, and cold inhuman
Came from the shore the wails of ancient women.
Descend like that old saint, patrician, wise
Driving the evil serpents with your eyes
Descend like him to aboriginal dark
And on the heart of evil set your mark,
Green-growing trefoil of immortal love,
See the black ravens scattered, and your dove
Garlanded with the sacred mistletoe
While the druid voices rise in anger, grow
Until the latin music drowns the sound.

The sacred maidens dance nor touch the ground
So light, so vibrant, so ethereally
Rose-petals blown upon an angry sea
This land remembers, must forever hold
Music of wind-wet silver, and that sense
Of low, subdued, and secret violence.
And the shawled women praying, the bare feet
The green-eyed children, ruddy, ragged, fleet

The emerald waters sheeted in green glass
The hills of shaded violet, green-black grass
And the faint odor of dissolving snow
When first the young buds on the blackthorn blow.

This aboriginal landscape, primitive
Drives me far westward where I cannot live
Oh, to the warmer, gentler, happier South
My soul draws closer, to relieve its drouth
Not this lost isle, this West that leans to North
Can I survive? I send this message forth
To you the bravest of survivors? Look and lean
From your high tower of vision, all is green
This land is in your blood, you will prefer
To be this chill's, this mist's, interpreter.

LANDSCAPE, FRUIT
AND FLOWERS

In lands of perpetual summer this fixed, miniature
    scene
Always the sunlight falls on orchards sloping seaward
Light from celestial worlds that brighten fruit and
    flowers
Untouched by frost, cold, snow
And Time's harsh overflow.

Seen only through consuming fever, convalescent glass
When our known landscape fades in arid hours
And the prisoner longs for this infallible view
In yards where nothing blooms, the starved senses turn
Burning into infinity and yearn
For this too luminous and unwithering grass.

Here flame the deep red roses known and plucked
Only by the heroic dead; green-veined against green
    vines
The heat-faint grapes recline, and the dark velvet
    plums
Wait for the harvester who never comes
Warm ripening that never meets the day
That lingers 'twixt fruition and decay.

Or it is a park scene, close-cut grass, cultivated walks
While overhead in golden classic heavens
Scream the white birds between the earth and sea
Uneasy warning in their cries, the roses rare as orchids
Hear them and fade, deep white on deep red grows
And a calm wind blows.

Summer's eternal garland, pastoral crown
Source of earth's deepest music sadly lingers
Peace and contentment smile
As if they knew this land was for an heir
Who saw this world through phantasies and dreams
Flashes of grief, illuminated gleams
And claimed no lot in his possessions there.

But left it to the white and gleaming marble
The sightless, impeccable Gods who guard the sunsets
And occasional visitors through fever freed
To see the imperishable skies of memory's isle.
Seen with their childhood's eyes, seen but by desperate
    men
Who would be born again.

VOYAGE

(FOR JOANNA)

Meet me where sky and air
Shine upon antique marble, heaven-drowned land
Where golden apples fade on the sea strand
And where the stone-eyed gods, severe and tall,
Loom white and mythical.

Where all is poised forever glazed and clear
Above the drugged, unmoving atmosphere,
Where the skies sleep in some intenser blue
Than any known to you,
Time's motion is arrested, there we'll spend
Our love to some wise end.

Unmoor the dreaming ships that swan-like float
Diaphanous and rapt on heavy waters—
What starry music from unearthly throat
Rises from opaque waves, oh, what king's daughter?
What lovely trouble trembles in the sound
It sings of other ships that met disaster
Sailing to the lost isles of alabaster,
Or Cytherea, or Atlantis bound?

Unmoor the ghostly boats and let us go
To ports that no men know.
The map is in my heart and you shall see
Wide seas unknown to your geography,
Yet real, real, real as memories of our race,
That place unknown where our beginnings trace
All love, all beauty and all force
To its lost source.

[23]

Pursued by demons, he
Leaves listening trees behind
The faintly ominous wind
Murmurs unceasingly;
He mounts his horse to ride
Out of the quick storm's reach.
Fear has a subtle speech
That is so low and kind
A ruined angel's face
And an envenomed mind
(Death sleeps in its embrace).

Rides fast into the wood
Where the masked stranger stood
Feels horror in his blood
And sees cloaked misery
Point with its fleshless hand
To the infested land:
Even the smallest blade
Of shuddering new grass
Unites in powerful shade
And will not let him pass.
All night wind-furies rave
Upon the blossoming grave
Of many a murdered man
But the remote sky sheds balm
In gentle cloudy rain
Slant coolness that can calm
The phantoms of his brain

Nor more is he accursed
Who has endured the worst.

Oh, the sweet rain, the dew
That must foretell the morn
And heaven's earliest blue
Now under gray eclipse
To ride for love's own sake
Into the weeping skies
Until the morning-break
Breathes coolness on his lips
And love across his eyes
He sees the young dawn arise
Pale on her silver bed
And light as fresh as springs
From mountain watershed
Pours from her opening wings.

THE RETURN

Return to terrible skies flecked by the storm
Return to sorrowing angels cast from heaven
Remember paradise and its perfect climate
Contract the summer storm, enter the breasts
Of love-lorn maidens ruffle their low sighing
And make the bed of marriage safe and warm.

Go dripping whiteness like small lakes of snow
Upon blanched air, grown ivory-pale with waiting
Sardonic mystery of the peaceful mind
Make parables for wit, rhymes for the lonely traveller
Disturb the child-mind like a near relation
Brooding in horror's pit, rise vast and grow.

Till innocence, spring, small poems, pink cherry blos-
    soms
Protected by your shadow, bloom new meanings
Neglected beauties bud grow gay and precious
Again the matron fastens the gold ear-rings
Light on her pretty ears, again the string of pearls
Makes whiter and more bright the May-time bosoms.

Spinets, harps, and guitars a welcome sing
Welcome O exiled dove, to lands destroyed by famine
Where cruel wrath profaned your gentle white,
Recall the romantic paradise, the demure, summer
    land
Where idyllic fountains streamed in milk, wine, honey
On silky air, the mild wind, and your wings sounding.

Welcome O dove, play musical white fingers
Sweeping with sweetness, on stringed instruments
The virgin hearts rejoice; through stained glass win-
dows
The choir lauds your charms in choicest latin
The naked Venus greets you in the garden
And on her marble limbs (O dove!) your shadow
lingers.

THE EMIGRES

Oh, in a harsh suspicious time,
Suspicious time
Metallic angry, dark with war
Disturbing every heritage
That once made gold the poet's page
To dream of pastoral days when rage
Comes like a sickness through the door
Brings but confusion; reveries
That are disease.

Yet guard your sibyllic books, oh, love
Preserve for love
Old prophecies of happiness
When the lamb sleeps beside the lion
And when the panther's unleashed grace
In tamed delight shall roam a place
In some forgotten paradise
Fruitful and ripe and evergreen
Unserpented, serene.

Blind outcasts from an age of steel,
The steel-sharp age
Knowing retreat is sacrilege
And brings its painful penalties
Of loneliness, unease
Yet hides for fear behind old marble
The armless Venus, eyeless Jove
The Apollo of the shattered lyre
The little battered god of love

And sees no ancient solace near
Only the stealthy feet of fear
Unchanging through the changing year,
The death-changed year.

Their wings are pointed with light, only in warmth
and the sun
Do their great pinions widen and circle the golden air
And lift their passionate heads bronze gold on the
glittering sky
Till the white glory of motion uplifts them they are
done
Poised in the steep, deep, dark on the emblazoned
stair.

Darkling, soft-studded on the skies vast blue
The timid stars arise with tender and innocent throats
And brilliant arrested faces answering them,
Invocation upon invocation, diadem upon diadem.

But in palaces of light and on the throne
Where the great vision sits, enrapt, alone
In that immense enduring solitude
Where every haunted and enchanted note
From each angelic throat
Is heard and loved; is understood and known.
The sun's bronze lamp is at last overthrown
For heavenly meditation and the stars
Resume their station in the sacred wood.

THE DREAM

In that rich burial ground where the levelled dead
Lie darkened in extinction, I have groped
Through solitudes like death, as hopeless, lonely.
The Gothic terror in suspended air,
The cemetery reached, I saw the flowers,
Live roots among the dead, blazing in dark
Red bloom on marble, purple on the tombs
Flushed in the light, like an expiring passion
No ghost, no shadow stirred.
The reassuring blood raced through my veins
Aware and deathless in the dead meadow
Stars, thick as clustered flowers, enriched the heavens.
And light as cold as ether tinted the tombs,
But at one tomb, the light fell down aslant:
"Approach, approach, and read, and know no more."

Through creeping moss I read my name, I know
My name obscured, my tomb the smallest there.
No cypress weeps, but the moon's steady eye
Brims on it with a studied, bright compassion,
Irrevocable as the spoken word, poignant as love.

DEATH IS THE SERPENT

This moment when the sun is ebbing slowly
And the hushed world retreats
I saw the danger approaching, the declining power
Of heat in my slow veins, the serpent coiled to spring
On the tired hour.

Death, the dark serpent, heavy-eyed and holy,
The expiring sunlight greets
God of the coming night in torment languishing
Till each decaying thing
Is purified in air, in rain, in fire.
It shall at last expire
When the young world shall send its new grass forth
And the new sun arise
To open the dead eyes.

AFTERNOON OF A DOLL

The mottled afternoon shall shade
Your face of wax, the pink, the ivory-colored
Beauty that charms with mediocrity
Our minds are pleased with easy comprehension.
Sit in your wicker chair, nor wind, nor shock
Nor the mind's darkness make your soul afraid;
Death in itself is but banality
When it breathes upon the fluffy, silver gold
Of your fine platinum-shining hair.
Let sunlight beat upon your exquisite frock.

When the toy drums go mute on tiny ears,
Reducing noise to its absurdity,
Let hobby horses, gay with wine-red saddles,
Prance for your motionless delight
And let the small boy, auburn-haired, green-eyed,
Display his reckless and equestrian pride
Before your daintiness, who sits and preens
In infinitesimal and waxen dreams.
Deride, deride the shrieking auto horns
That blare through city windows, traffic lights
Red, green, green, red through window screens,
And the harsh voices rising from the city
Without reverence, and without pity.

TRANSIENT, BRIGHT FLOWER

This is the time of darkening wind and tide,
The time, oh, reaper of the sea's large waste!
Rain desolate, wave-racked and ocean-maimed,
To wander out in mist, glad as a bride,
To meet the storm's last ominous sound, the sea-bird's
    haste,
To gather, like the queen dark Pluto claimed
Against the perilous brink, the flowers so small, so
    few,
The transient beauty, startling and new.

Possess your arms with brief and fragile bloom,
This austere luxury of the frugal year,
A warmth transcending the gray atmosphere
Will light bright candles in your mind's chill room.
And sing your songs, white girls whose milky feet
Wade in the streams of morning where the dew
Is iridescent, dream-entranced as you.
Sing against rocky winds and wavering skies
Until the wing of darkness faints and dies,
Such songs as rise from music's subtlest spring,
Her murmuring wells of water untapped, clear
Against the onslaughts of the desperate year,
Sunny and crystal glittering without stain;
Walk through the wavering clouds, the diminishing
    rain
And see secluded, shy through lessening shower,
The world's reward, the bright, the transient flower.

THE POSSESSED

Hallucination does its part
Nourished on bitter hours
It grows incarnate in the heart
And breeds supernal flowers.

Kept warm in brooding's thinnest silk
It grows in strength and hardihood
Within its veins the body's milk
Corrupts the flesh and blood.

The vultures eat our eyes, a snake
Uncoils and sings
Of a large burning lake
That cools the sharpest stings.

Sinking we see the glittering spires
Of lost cathedrals, valleys wooing
The wind, fulfilled desires.
Hear shadowy wood doves cooing.

On cottages built in the air
Where no man loves, where no man dwells
Unbodied voices hover there
In false hosannas and farewells.

THE VIRGIN, THE DOE
AND THE LEPER

They are always there
The frightened virgin at the burning fountain
The leper left upon the fatal stair
The milk-white doe lost on the savage mountain.

Do you not hear them cry?
Despair and shame that final sense
Of doom descending upon innocence
Outcasts from pity's gentle eye?

I fly their shadowy pain
I invoke the guardians of their destiny
Angels of thunder and rain
To keep sick pity from corrupting me.

Earth would deny them
As I deny and plead, earth pleads, denies
"O pitiful, stain not my garment's hem
And hide from me the silent wound that bleeds."

For are we not lost too?
Are we not outcasts from time's living flood?
And often from the sky's deceptive blue
Rains down a shower of blood.

When shelter seemed most near, and love most close
When summer's golden eyelids opened wide
Have we not seen the worm crawl from the rose
Have we not seen the shadowy sisters glide?

Fatal and wan on cherished garden walks
Whose was that sudden cry? that burning chill?
What halts our footsteps? and what stilled our talks?
What shadow stalks us, run wherever we will?

THE RESPITE

Plunged into silence like a desperate swimmer
I leap in icy waves and feel the tides
Rise with a flowing sigh, a violent shock
Parting the waters; then the strong sun enters
On the drenched limbs, that slowly float away
Speech is the water, sun is silence.

Therefore I now resign O obdurate tides
My difficult speech whose meanings cold and rocky
Give joy to none; too soon the wind and wave
Carry the words away, stun the fine edge of meaning
Like a strong wave the clearer sunlight falls
I rest in the white shade of soundless peace.

See! on the drifting spars of life you float
Ophelia-garlanded with early flowers
The gray devouring sea shall rot away.
Open your eyes now strong to bear the sun
Limbs glazed by pale, green waves, your thin hands
    empty
Quiet, relaxed, upon the moving waters.

Now you are pierced with the calm solitude
Pierced through the heart with death and still rejoic-
    ing
Now faints on salty air that speech sea-drenched
And on the drooping lashes the pearl tear
Dissolves in joy, that terrible joy when pain
Dies in exhaustion and respite is quiet
Silence surrounds you.

[38]

Only your eyes will speak, only your floating body
Resigned in storm that carries you away
To latitudes of silence vast and lonely
Gone is the season when the musical leaves
Measured their watery syllables on dry air
And the earth spoke in the brief speech of flowers.

Perfectly, unearthly clear
Ebbs away the dying year;
Snowfall, windstorm, and the rain
Freezing on the window pane.
Warm the little world within
But the body grown too thin
Shrinks before the leaping gold
Fire that blazes sharp as cold
Hyacinth the shadows fall
Blend with gold lights on the wall
Evening like dulled water spills
Snowy silver on the hills.

Thought and legend now keep warm
This world of shadow and of storm
Silent sister, Amor's bride
Gleaming shadow at my side,
Let your honeyed legend stand
Between me and the winter land
Half defined its meanings flash
Fine as the hair of an eyelash
O sweet the final days to spend
With Love and Love's most cherished friend
Who from her mortal reverie
Rose in her young antiquity
Dewy, bright, and evergreen
She haunts the passing winter scene.

Psyche, sister, when we go
In longer winters, whiter snow
And phantasy and fire give birth
To deeper meanings of the earth
In wisdom, courage, and resolve
All seasons into snow dissolve
And as we know the ultimate pang
Far out of time the great bells clang
Heavy and loud, but you most bright
Psyche clear and spirit-light
As a child's breath, clear brookwater
Amor's love, the Cyprian's daughter
Solace, oh, fly before me where
The deathvoice stains the glassy air.

THE ECHO

Echo herself tuned all his art
Hers was the music, hers the plaint
Hollow and false and sweetly faint
Of the great music's classic part
As if a lover half afraid
Ran to embrace a wavering golden shade.

Whose long and perilous locks untied
Warm in the lovesick air float free
It was her light that smote the sea
This wandering gold on earth and tide
That every falling shadow mocks
Wooing her authentic voice, her unrivaled locks.

Now lost forever he must seek
The cypher to her inmost thought
Almost (ah, almost) found and caught
The vision obsolete and Greek
Sharp music of her far off lute
That half denies, but never spurns his suit.

Echoes from seawater and air
Din in his ears with futile cries
The world grows heavy with his sighs
The early heavens fade in care
The cold rocks sound with his lament
And with his grief the sun and moon are spent.

Spent is the sun and thinned the gold
Of hope's rich coin, slow-worn, once bright
Yet his beloved one winter night
Visited him when deadly cold
Descended on his despairing heart
Came to his bed, unveiled her face, revealed her art.

Opened her arms, and bared her throat
Interpreted her mysteries
Simple, profound as growing trees
That in starred waters seem to float
All night she sang like an expiring swan
That floats with joyous pain into the rising dawn.

With wide cool eyes she gazes on mankind
And through its eyes her inward sweetness looks
Mirror-reflected. All dark thoughts refined
Purified as in a thousand mountain brooks.

Her own face seems mankind's, young, kind, dew-clear
Transformed by deepsea music it has heard
Her voice strained sweet and cold; in atmosphere
Like after rain, warm colors washed and blurred.

She knows the world is joy's and she can bless
Each day to come with a rich miracle
And draw time to her in a swift caress
While music flows from some fresh-rising well.

But time has ceased to breathe upon her glass
And when she looks she sees another face
Rise from behind the mirrored wilderness
With frantic arms outstretched for an embrace.

Face of a scarecrow sorrow-worn and sick
Emaciated, pale, a death's head way
Of smiling. Limbs loose, eyes of a lunatic.

Grosser than dust, a little less than clay.

THE RUNAWAY

Silent and stealthy days that hour by hour
Spring up unnoticed as a flower
In summer grass; and like a breath, a light, a feather
Make my world's weather.
I wished to weave a garland, deep and rare,
To wear upon my hair,
Or a long chain, intricate, strong and fine
To sound through stillness and to shine,
To bind the intangible days that so efface
Themselves with me, and run so dull a pace.
O they have run! they have gone! nor have they set
Their seal of vast regret
Upon that wide and echoing door
That, opening, opens, shuts and sounds no more.
How to pursue Life's Runaway? let go
The innumerable sands that through my fingers flow?
Forgo the moons and waters of the mind:
Today is all that you shall find.

When shall the broken carvèd wings
Rise whole and exquisite?
The obscured pathos of forgotten things
There in archaic charm I saw him sit
The multiple Eros of each clime

Upon an iron base
Heavy with the dull sift of time
Dust on his rounded face
The little dimples on his cheek and chin
Drew stony hearts within.
His crisply curling hair,
Where no winds stir,
Even in neglect presents
Such infant innocence
That the heart weeps for a caress.
Oh, to his dusty breast I crept
And on the stone as if on lilies slept,
And in my sleep received
The wound now unrelieved
The wound for which no balm
Restores the piercèd heart
Restores the careless calm
And there is no redress.
Still is this altar Love's and still divine
Even from his broken dart
Even from his ruined shrine
Such fire, such terror, and such bliss will start. . . .

Oh, touch his frozen lips
That dew of ages sips
And press them to your own
Though his are carved of stone
See from the trembling shrine an air uncloses
Breathing of sunlight and dissolvèd roses
Though pale the roses, brief the light
They bloom, they shine, in darkest night.

This face no crystal is, the clearest glass
Obscures the entrance of the sun
Through the fine-textured flesh, the blood will run
But lets the large communication pass
The mind no window is,
For the last meaning, but it holds the rays
Of worlds more great than this
That hover as a shadow on our days
And stains the perfect light with dusty blur
Makes all uncertain that was clear before
Something escapes, unknown
More like a sigh, a flower, a slight twig thrown
Against the sky's transparent mirror cast
By face, by mind, by living image made
Part sunlight and part shade.

Since neither glass nor God's white thought you are,
How can you hope to hold the expiring sand
Or measure the fine meaning of a star
Or trace the Mount of Saturn on your hand
Or follow the fluid flight of anything
That mounts to heaven on feather-arrowed wing?
In the wide air of silence, wondering
Say to your soul, "Oh soul you are unfit
To read this brief life's meaning or to guess
This secret, individual, loneliness"
But ripen in the dark, swell in the moving air
Till time supplies the final requisite,
Breathe in the numbered hairs upon my head
Until the beckoning image on the stair
Dissolves confusion and dispels our dread.

ANGEL-INFANCY

In the cool corridors in the still room,
In the dark watches of the endless day
I see his delicate wings, the innocent eyes
Of the unborn love, restless within my brain
The light, the childish form takes life again.

Winged with a softness quicker than April air,
Garlanded with flowers whose fragrance time nor
    change
Nor revolution of the sun can mar,
Snow-calm, rose-lovely, violet-sweet,
Are his unearthbound feet.

Oh, darling miracle in whom the world
Restores its idyllic dream, its golden age,
Mysterious-simple as the living grass
Or the arched quiet of the growing trees,
Or the reserved, full-blown white peonies.

Oh, filled with overflowing,
The fountain brimmed with love:
The heart is not slaked
Nor the fire quenched.

Nor is the fever stayed.
The vehement fire must lie
On flames that have no ending
In hunger and in thirst.

The tall tree ever-growing
In the forsaken rock
Blossoms in Aprils that no eye can see,
Yet in its shade,
Lovely in solitude
Where the wild deer stood,
Shake leaf and blossom.

So the wild heart
Under no foliage, in no fountain
Finds the desired solace
Too deep the crystal,
Too sparse the tree.

Under no mountain
Is the beloved shade;
On no soft turf
Is made that bed
Foreseen by longing.

THE TIDE

As break the ocean tides on the worn stone,
Valedictory and wan, the morning hours
Dissolve in spray and leave the world alone
Save for the trees' wide bliss, the sudden flowers;

Save for the expectant shadow in my mind
That hopes and trembles fearing to be born
To unaccustomed light and troubling wind,
The sun's derision and the season's scorn.

White tides of heaven, rise until the sea
And sky unite in purging the still thought
Which has deprived me of serenity
And left me trembling, white and overwrought.

Dissolve the mist, dissolve the impious fear
That mars the tide, profanes the patient trees,
Discolors the transparent atmosphere
Until I wade in terror to my knees.

So on one night he came,
And left upon my breast
Engraved in sharpest flame,
The words on which I rest.

The seasons and the sky
Grew far too still and clear
Who heard the trumpet cry
In that heroic year.

The broken bread, the wine
Whose simple mystery
Man's curious thoughts refine
Into a vaster law
I saw.

Till the small house took light
And shone enlarged and tall
In every glittering wall
That faced the night.

For that prized messenger,
Who for a little while
Revealed his haunted face,
I write, I shape my style.

And let it be as pure
As that unearthly brow
Whose words I study now
And keep secure.

To love the truth, to shield
Its hard and lonely way,
To choose the stark defeat,
Rather than seek retreat
When it is well to yield.

RENEWAL OF FOUNTAINS

Bright universe unseen, yet seen awhile,
Precious and brief in a tree bathed in light
And in shy, sudden flowers
In rain, in hasty storm.

Or where the air is moist with trancèd heat
Under the noonday sun remote and high
We wander and are lost
In golden-shadowy lanes.

Or in the hyacinth shadows of the night
Where the black hills' immaculate, warm line
Meets with translucent blue
And the dark waters run.

With silver-pointed stars for company,
Light-tipped, soft-shaded, deep, the world revolves
To eloquent bright eyes
That pierce through shade.

All this endures, revives and calms the mind
When the harsh day is done, the bitter wars
And winter's icy voice
Chills sky and air.

Here, waiting for renewal, fountains play,
Sparkling, inviting, dancing and withdrawn
Hope withers and is green,
Destroyed, restored.

Wanderer in intricate paths, bewildered soul,
When all that pleased you once shall please no more,
Rest and desire no rest
Under the common grass.

While summer's loosened sun-enamoured hair
And bright abstracted green
Pallor, and starry sheen
Envelop us as the warm seasons fade
Into a cooler shade.
Then flows upon the lawn
The golden signal, the red leaf, the autumn's mes-
    senger
Glad Goddess winged with morning and cloud-born
Whose snowy feet the celestial meadows stir
Herald this day with russet, yellow and brown
And in full season scatter the harvest down
While deepening thought on the calmed heaven
    grows.

Dispelled is the wild legend of the rose
But light pours from the heaven, hopes fall from the
    sky
Strange the migrating birds' departing cry
And softly, lightly, now less ardently
We face a world robbed of the sun's glare
Now with the heart to see
Not with the blinded brain
Nor with the limited eyes' impassioned stare
Too weak to pierce the growing mystery
Of time, and change, and the fast withering tree.

INDIAN SUMMER

Rumors of heaven, lost, regained, restored
Are on the air today, quickening and delaying
The blood's pulse, and the heart's tremor
Where once Corinna had gone out a-maying,
Her apron full of blossoms of celestial color
The rich tart apples rosy and sharp to taste,
Fall on the withering grass in profuse haste,
A delectable squandering, a precious waste.

Now the cool blossoms have the sheen of metal,
The warmth, the silken texture stiffens and hardens
And silver light veins each imperturbable petal.
You, too, Corinna, have grown silent and whiter,
No longer on light grass your swift feet tarry
Breaking the pauses with a wild rose laughter
The sun at your shoulder, bright clouds speeding after.

And all the heavens are pale and thin-veined blue,
Peers through escaping light too timidly,
The message runs in signals through the door,
Of each time-silenced house, the window panes
Reflect the burden of the wind's descent
What mighty messenger, sky-shadowed lightning
        sent,
Runs in cold daylight through leaf-scattered lanes,
Murmuring of falling leaves, sky's discontent?

THE WARNING

The inward eye consumes the flesh
Alive upon the fragile frame
Rivers of living blood run dry
And perish under sterile flame.
The new, the vigorous, the fresh
Endure no more; the seasons sigh
As if perpetual autumn fell
On a green field and gathered up
Summer and warmth, and joy and health
And drank in one deep poisoned cup
A full life's richest wine by stealth.

Reach outward, spirit-tendrils, grow
To the sun's eye, the lustier green
That shines for all eyes and is seen.
Avoid that secret, silent glow,
Unhealthy subtle of the moon
That drains the living world away
And frets to shade the light of day
And that intense platonic swoon
In starrier heavens and more bright
Than earth's small fire, oh, heart, beware
The unearthly bliss, the lunar light
The phantom on the burning stair.

SEASON IN SNOW

See how the declining year disrobes itself of light
The green, the ruddy gold, the sunny blue
To the fixed seasons true;
The rose fades from the hour, dissolves in cloudy
    white
White, white, the beautiful hour silent and white
Immure our lives in changing atmosphere
The cold descends like brightness from the air
Fair, rare, the aging year grows white and fair
With the stripped garlands on her windblown hair.

Let us sing Winter, the fair unbeloved:
Only the fastidious mind is finally moved
To love her naked, bleak, and delicate line
When time's fixed touch is careful to refine
The chill and difficult world where loveliness
Divests herself of her rose-bordered dress.

And waits on memory, sees closed rivers sleep
Follows the frozen clouds' authentic fleece
With large doomed eyes of peace
And sees the cool, bright-plumaged wings of the snow
And men with muffled footsteps walking slow.

That great desire for waters ever flowing,
Cooling and deep, oh, soft, oh, willow-shaded,
Never fulfilled. How fresh the waters run
Under perpetual April, under such a sun
Brightness falling on new grass, light-green and ever
blowing.

Dear dream, diminishing and still more sweet
As the years waver, dwindle and retreat,
Open my eyes at last, at last to see
The city trees, lost, hard and sharp and true,
The blossoms stunted and the fruit, how few.
Stone under feet, the stony skies descend
Harsh and impersonal, greet as a friend
The rocky morning and the brazen noon,
The desperate evening clothed in metal stars
And so resume your wars.

'Twixt shrinking flesh and willing spirit stands
The invincible sword on whom all victory waits,
Between the desolation and the fates
Run only living waters and the cool
Spring-waving grass remains, the heaven-drowned
flowers endure,
Breaking through city pavements, crystal and pure.

Remembering one day when your wide eyes
Opened to startle me for the first time,
Undedicated moment, did the tree
That bears futurity burst into bloom
With lovelier flowers than we could realize?

The roar, the thunder of the barbaric city,
Thunder that poured its heat in heart, in head
Grew mild with tenderness and soft with pity,
What happy rumour woke the unhappy dead?

The sacred moment fades, but thought is long:
Oh, unbelievable, believe, say you believe
Only in miracles, only in what comes to pass
In the dark midnight when the lost souls grieve
And the long twilight hides the summer grass.

That which is lost is found, the tenuous beauty snared,
The fine, the golden note caught and repeated:
Oh, how it rings on the ear, wild-sweet, round and
    completed.

FLOWERING LAUREL

The laurels are not cut,
"The flowering laurel tree
Blooms once again for thee";
Your windows all are shut.

Escaping luxury,
No more shall be restored
The delicate petalled hour
That burst into a flower,
Crisp-white and red,
And lifted its slight head
Unnoticed, unadored.

Return, return, white shower,
Rose shower, and ivory sheen
Glowing through deepest green,
Frail substance veined with power
Bloom, blossom, bask in the sun
Before you are undone.

Before the moon's dead pallor
Obscures the living light
And the day's beauties pine,
Drooping in hopeless valor,
And are withdrawn from sight.
Be landscape, fruit, and vine
Oh, for a while, be mine!